Other books by Exley:
Flowers a Celebration   Garden Lover's Book of Days
Country Notebook   Garden Lover's Quotations
Flower Lover's Birthday Book   Flower Arranging Address Book

Published simultaneously in 1993 by Exley Publications
in Great Britain, and Exley Giftbooks in the USA.
Selection and arrangement © Helen Exley 1993.

ISBN 1-85015-283-7

A copy of the CIP data is available from the British Library on request.

Edited by Helen Exley.
Text research by Margaret Montgomery.
Designed by Pinpoint Design.
Picture research by P. A. Goldberg and J. Clift / Image Select, London.
Typeset by Delta, Watford.
Printed and bound by William Clowes, Beccles, UK.
Exley Publications Ltd, 16 Chalk Hill, Watford, Herts WD1 4BN, U.K.
Exley Giftbooks, 359 East Main Street, Suite 3D, Mount Kisco, NY 10549, USA.

Text credits: Dr Stefan Buczacki, extract from *Three Men in a Garden*, published
by BBC Books; Eleanor Farjeon, "June's Song", from *The Children's Bells*,
published by Oxford University Press; H.L.V. Fletcher, extract from *The Rose
Anthology*, published by George Newnes, 1963; Roy Genders, extracts from *The
Rose. A Complete Handbook*, published by Robert Hale; Princess Grace, extracts
from *My Book of Flowers*, published by Sidgwick & Jackson, London, 1980 and
Doubleday, New York; Susan Hill, extracts from *Through the Garden Gate*,
published by Hamish Hamilton, extract from *The Magic Apple Tree*, published by
Penguin 1982; Malcolm Hillier, extract from *The Little Scented Library: Roses*,
published by Dorling Kindersley, London and Simon & Schuster, New York;
E. J. Howard, extract from *Green Shades*, published by Aurum Press, 1991;
Deborah Kellaway, extract from *For Love of a Rose*, published by Faber & Faber,
1965; David Squire with Jane Newdick, extract from *The Book of the Rose*,
published by Crescent Books, a division of Random House Inc, New York;
Geoffrey Smith, extracts from *A Passion for Plants*, published by David &
Charles, 1990; Vita Sackville-West, extract from *Vita Sacville-West's Garden
Book*, ©Nigel Nicolson, 1968, published by Michael Joseph.
Picture credits: Chris Beetles, London: page 8; Bridgeman Art Library: title
pages and pages 11, 19, 24, 31, 34, 38, 40, 44, 50, 53, 57; Christies, London: page
31; Fine Art Photographic Library: cover and pages 13, 21, 23, 26, 33, 42, 46, 59;
Giraudon, Paris: pages 15, 17, 28, 54, 60/61; Guildhall Art Gallery, London: page
38; Images/Horizon: 7, 37; Roy Miles Gallery, London: page 19; Musee d'Art
Ancien, Paris: page 54; ©Beatrice Parsons "Our Lady's Flowers", page 51; ©
Minnie Smythe "Rose Border", page 56; ©John Wilkinson, pages 7, 37;
Christopher Wood Gallery, London: pages 51, 24, 56, 11, 34; York City Art
Gallery: page 53.

ROSES

A CELEBRATION
IN WORDS
AND PAINTINGS

SELECTED BY
HELEN EXLEY

EXLEY
MT. KISCO, NEW YORK • WATFORD, UK

THE COMING OF SPRING

...the White-thorn, lovely May,
Opens her many lovely eyes listening; the Rose
still sleeps,
None dare to wake her; soon she bursts her
crimson-curtain'd bed
And comes forth in the majesty of beauty...

WILLIAM BLAKE (1757-1827)

Each rose that comes brings me greetings from
the Rose of an eternal spring.

RABINDRANATH TAGORE (1861-1941)

When [old roses] are all out, at midsummer,
the sight is so joyous, the scent so abundant,
that one can only laugh and say; "*Look* at the
roses!" Or perhaps someone says: "The roses
are specially good this year." But they have
forgotten: the roses are good every year.

DEBORAH KELLAWAY

THE BEST FLOWER OF ALL

No flower is better known or more commonly found than the rose, none has such a romantic place in literature, symbol of love and youthful sweetness, beauty and death. No garden is complete without one, no plant is more obliging, versatile, various, full of charm, none can be so delightful or so dull, so easy and yet so temperamental.

SUSAN HILL,
FROM *"THROUGH THE GARDEN GATE"*

Of all the cultivated flowers, the rose is pre-eminent, the most recognized, collected, grown and hybridized - used for decoration, in painting, in sculpture, in embroidery, for perfume, in poetic imagery. Throughout the world, and for thousands of years, the rose has held us in mystic thrall.

E. J. HOWARD,
FROM *"GREEN SHADES"*

BANKS OF ROSES

In a Rose-garden...no formalism, no flatness, no monotonous repetition, should prevail. There should the Rose be seen in all her multiform phases of beauty. There should be beds of Roses, banks of Roses, bowers of Roses, hedges of Roses, edgings of Roses, pillars of Roses, arches of Roses, fountains of Roses, baskets of Roses, vistas and alleys of the Rose. Now overhead and now at our feet, there they should creep and climb. New tints, new forms, new perfumes, should meet us at every turn.

S. REYNOLDS HOLE

And the roses - the roses! Rising out of the grass, tangled round the sun-dial, wreathing the tree-trunks, and hanging from their branches, climbing up the walls ... with long garlands falling in cascades - they came alive day by day, hour by hour. Fair, fresh leaves, and buds - and buds - spilling themselves over their brims and filling the garden air.

FRANCES HODGSON-BURNETT

WOVEN THROUGH MY LIFE

The first flowers I can remember were two different roses. I was very small and it was a long time ago.

The years seem to filter from our childhood memories all except that which was beautiful and happy and gay so that the roses I remember were probably the finest and loveliest I shall ever know.

I grow both these roses myself today, but, treasured as they are, and unwilling as I am to admit it, sometimes the colours are not quite so deep, the perfume not so delicate and lingering.

You can see the exquisite shades for the first time, smell the delicious scent for the first time, only once in a lifetime. So there will never be roses quite, *quite,* as good ever again.

H.L.V. FLETCHER,
FROM *"THE ROSE ANTHOLOGY"*

Cutting great sheaves of HT and floribunda roses in the early morning with the cool of night still in them was one of my duties during the six years I spent working in a large private garden. To be made free of a lovely garden in the cool, fresh intimate quiet of what, in memory, were near perfect summer mornings, added a specially rich pattern to the tapestry flowers have woven through my life.

GEOFFREY SMITH

ROSES ALL THE WAY

You love the roses - so do I. I wish
The sky would rain down roses, as they rain
From off the shaken bush. Why will it not?
Then all the valley would be pink and white
And soft to tread on. They would fall as light
As feathers, smelling sweet: and it would be
Like sleeping and yet waking, all at once.

GEORGE ELIOT (MARY ANN EVANS) (1819-1880)

❧ ☙

Queen Cleopatra once had a whole lake
scattered with rose petals to impress her guests.
When she set the scene in which to woo Marc
Antony, she had an entire floor covered with
rose petals up to twelve inches deep (some
historians even say eighteen) over which a net
was stretched. To reach her rose-strewn chaise
longue, he had to pick his way over this
heavenly scented mattress of petals. The effect,
alas, has not been recorded by history.

PRINCESS GRACE OF MONACO (1929-1982)

❧ ☙

Over the garden walls roses rambled in profusion, it being almost possible to touch their huge trusses as one passed along the road. Town and countryside were ablaze with beauty which far outshone the almost feeble attempt to gain recognition by other flowers. It was roses all the way, and the sun shone on their beauty and their fragrance pervaded the atmosphere, fanned by the gentle warm summer breeze.

ROY GENDERS

If Zeus chose us a King of the flowers in his
mirth,
He would call to the rose and would royally
crown it,
For the rose, ho, the rose! is the grace of the earth,
Is the light of the plants that are growing upon it.
For the rose, ho, the rose! is the eye of the flowers,
Is the blush of the meadows that feel
themselves fair, –
Is the lightning of beauty, that strikes through
the bowers
On pale lovers who sit in the glow unaware.
Ho, the rose breathes of love! ho, the rose lifts
the cup
To the red guest of Cyprus invoked for a guest!
Ho, the rose having curled its sweet eaves for
the world,
Takes delight in the motion its petals keep up,
As they laugh to the Wind as it laughs from
the West.

ELIZABETH BARRETT BROWNING (1806-1861),
"SONG OF THE ROSE" **(ATTRIBUTED TO SAPPHO)**

❦ ❦

Enter, then, the Rose-garden when the first sunshine sparkles in the dew, and enjoy with thankful happiness one of the loveliest scenes of earth. What a diversity, and yet what a harmony, of colour! There are White Roses, Striped Roses, Blush Roses, Pink Roses, Rose Roses, Carmine Roses, Crimson Roses, Scarlet Roses, Vermilion Roses, Maroon Roses, Purple Roses, Roses almost Black, and Roses of a glowing gold. What a diversity, and yet what a harmony, of outline! Dwarf Roses and Climbing Roses, Roses that droop to earth like fountains, and Roses that stretch out their branches upwards as though they would kiss the sun; Roses "in shape no bigger than an agate stone on the fore-finger of an alderman," and Roses four inches across; Roses in clusters, and Roses blooming singly; Roses in bud, in their glory, decline, and fall. And yet all these glowing tints not only combine, but educe and enhance each the other's beauty.... And over this perfect unity what a freshness, fragrance, purity, splendour!

S. REYNOLDS HOLE

❧ ❧

Perfume starts in the green parts of the plant, and its ingredients are light from the sun, carbon dioxide from the air, and the plant's own water....

The workings of the plant's perfumery in making sufficient raw materials in its green parts, conveying them to the petals on schedule, and conducting an intricate laboratory process within a swiftly growing and fragile material are marvellous indeed. The perfumery is only one industry within the green skin of a plant, for also in the making are colours and pollen and ovules, to name but a few, all to be initiated and placed in working order at precise times and places...

Efforts have been made to analyse rose perfumes, which is an interesting study with some long words in it. But when we come down to it, all that matters to us right now is to know which are the most fragrant roses for our enjoyment...I will give you mine by sweetness more than by strength.

JACK HARKNESS

❦ ❧

LIFE'S GIFT

People from a planet without flowers would think we must be mad with joy the whole time to have such things about us.

IRIS MURDOCH, b.1919

❧ ❦

Our highest assurance of the goodness of providence seems to me to rest in the flowers. All other things, our desires, our food, are really necessary for our existence in the first instance. But this rose is an extra. Its smell and its colour are an embellishment of life, not a condition of it. It is only goodness which gives extras, and so I say again that we have much to hope for from the flowers.

SIR ARTHUR CONAN DOYLE (1859-1930)

❧ ❦

All the world glows with roses, roses, roses.

SAUL CHERNIHOVSKY (1875-1943)

❧ ❦

Once a year the gardener at the Hall took him over the rose-garden. It was a day to remember for the old man.

Here he wandered, sniffed, and lovingly fingered to his heart's content - speechless with admiration - dumb with delight. To the old man it was his idea of what heaven would be like.

C. VOSS-BARK,
FROM *"MY GARDEN'S GOOD-NIGHT"*

So, if it is to be a rose-garden, do not choose those stunted, unnatural earth-loving strains, which have nothing of vigour and wildness in them, nor banish other flowers which may do homage to the beauty of a rose as courtiers to a queen. Let climbing roses drop in a veil from the terrace and smother with flower-spangled embroidery the garden walls, run riot over vaulted arcades, clamber up lofty obelisks of leaf-tangled trellis, twine themselves round the pillars of a rose-roofed temple, where little avalanches of sweetness shall rustle down at a touch and the dusty gold of the sunshine shall mingle with the summer snow of flying petals. Let them leap in a great bow or fall in a creamy cataract to a foaming pool of flowers. In the midst of the garden set a statue of Venus with a great bloom trained to her hand, or of Flora, her cornucopia overflowing with white rosettes, or a tiny basin where leaden *amorini* seated upon the margin are fishing with trailing buds.

SIR GEORGE SITWELL

ROUNDING THE WORLD

Walk amongst your roses as the air cools at the close of a hot June day and share silent communion with the unrecorded thousands who down the centuries have done the same.

GEOFFREY SMITH,
FROM *"A PASSION FOR PLANTS"*

...roses in bloom are like music, they need no interpreter, they reach out beyond all barriers of race and language.

ANTONIA RIDGE,
FROM *"FOR LOVE OF A ROSE"*

What is a nation?
Just the same old garden
With a different name,
It may be here, it may be there
We grow the same roses everywhere.

REGINALD ARKELL

Gather ye rosebuds while ye may,
  Old Time is still a-flying:
And this same flower that smiles today
  Tomorrow will be dying.

ROBERT HERRICK (1591-1674)

Go lovely Rose,
Tell her that wastes her time and me,
That now she knows,
When I resemble her to thee
How sweet and fair she seems to be.

Tell her that's young,
And shuns to have her Graces spy'd,
That hadst thou sprung
In Deserts, where no men abide,
Thou must have uncommended died.

Then die, that she
The common fate of all things rare
May read in thee,
How small a part of time they share,
That are so wondrous sweet and fair.

EDMUND WALLER (1608-1687)

⇟ ⇞

Oh, this is the joy of the rose:
That it blows,
And goes.

WILLA CATHER (1873-1947)

⇟ ⇞

MESSENGER

The rose scents all history - crowns lovers, is strewn before brides and heroes, glows in the torchlight of a thousand festivals, falls in a rain of petals on a thousand cavalcades, is gathered in the arms of saints, is symbol of love and of eternity, symbol of earthly kingdoms and of the Queen of Heaven.

It shelters the dead in a gentle coverlet. It brings hope to the weary heart.

It speaks for the silent - is the messenger of love and longing.

It is passion, triumph, glory.

It is the gift of one heart to another.

PAM BROWN, b.1928

The rose reigns supreme over all the other flowers in the plant kingdom.

It has always held an important place in literature and legend, romance and everyday life, art and fashion.

From Roman times when baskets of rose

petals were strewn ankle deep for the delight of emperors and their guests, to the rose as the humble ingredient of scented recipes and sumptuous perfumes, this special flower has twined and blossomed its way through history like no other.

DAVID SQUIRE WITH JANE NEWDICK,
FROM *"THE BOOK OF THE ROSE"*

❧ ❦

THE IMMORTAL ROSE

...the rose, ancient or modern, lacks certain qualities that in any other plant would be considered essential. Majesty of stature, elegance of contour, and perennial interest. A rosebush out of flower is a nothing, and after pruning a less than nothing landscape of cut stumps and a horse manure mulch. Yet still roses enjoy near universal acclaim as the epitome of excellence in more than garden terms.

The reason why is not hard to find, it is identifying the qualities which is impossible. To walk in a garden with roses in full bloom is to discover some part of the answer. The flowers have a velvet-textured quality that gives a depth to petal colour in which the eye becomes immersed. Fragrance distilled from the flowers when they are warmed by the sun spills out in such abundance that on still, calm evenings the garden is filled with the refreshing perfume. The qualities are the same whether the garden is in Portland (Oregon), Paris, Lyon, St Albans

or Aberdeen, for roses are not of one nation or
any single period in history, they are timeless.
Possibly this is the secret that they have
gathered for themselves through the slow
passage of centuries - an extraordinary quality
which makes them immortal.

GEOFFREY SMITH,
FROM *"A PASSION FOR PLANTS"*

❧ ❧

SUMMER IN SURREY

The roses billow and blow.
Crimson and gold and round as peonies
they surge about the steps and flow
in waves of bloom
that lap about my feet
- too opulent for this well-ordered street
- a foam of blossom drowning every house,
bewitching all the suburb to a bower
and darkening my room:
a screen of glittering leaf and flower,
a scented gloom.

And men returning from the city wade
through depths of heavy-scented shade
or like spent swimmers drift ashore
before each neatly-numbered door
to drowse away the summer hours
marooned upon a reef of flowers.

PAM BROWN, b.1928

A <u>ROSE</u> FOR <u>MY</u> LOVE

Lovers now send a single silken rose, perfumed
and sealed into a plastic shell.
Is love so desperate to fend off change?
Better a rose still wet with rain, smelling of
summer and ephemeral. Speaking of living
love. Speaking of other summers yet to come.

PAM BROWN, b.1928

I bring you my rose.
It is a golden flame.
   Is Love its name?
It is a scarlet fire.
   Is it desire?
'Tis the white ash of coal.
   Is it the soul?
One, none, or all of those,
   I bring you my rose.

ELEANOR FARJEON (1881-1965)

And I will make thee beds of roses,
and a thousand fragrant posies.

CHRISTOPHER MARLOWE (1564-1593),
FROM *"A PASSIONATE SHEPHERD TO HIS LOVE"*

They [old roses] give you perfume beyond compare. They give you divine simplicity of bloom; the singles are the queen bees, chosen from the countless workers of the hedgerow roses while the doubles have none of the sculptured perfection that so pleases the show-bench judge. They are large and loose, shaggy and carefree. They shake their heads and shed their petals with all the nonchalance you would expect of a flower that has seen more suns than you or I ever will. Many of them are fleeting but, to my mind, none the worse for that. How much more do I treasure a plant that displays its glory for a few wonderful weeks than one that continuously thrusts forth flush after flush of production-line perfection. But the old roses have one thing most of all that elevates them above the earthly world of my other garden flowers; they have history. To sit on a balmy summer's evening and drink in the beauty of a rose that the Elizabethans saw puts a little magic into my gardening.

DR. STEFAN BUCZACKI,
FROM *"THREE MEN IN A GARDEN"*

&

I have been warned off old roses by a lot of people. They are prone to every disease, I am told, temperamental and touchy, scarcely worth the trouble. Old roses have character, and romance lingering in their pasts. They are like faded old beauties of Victorian and Edwardian country houses. I love their names and their rarity and the way they are ever so slightly blousy and yet paper-frail, too....I doubt if I shall ever be able to achieve the old rose garden I dream of, but I shall make a start....Old roses, alba roses, tea and damask and moss roses, most of them richly scented, many of them white or pink, which I prefer to reds and mauves. Belle de Crécy, Duchesse d'Angoulême, Félicité Parmentier, Madame Hardy, Wife of Bath, Mousseline, Old Pink Moss, all of them will have a place.... Albertine, of course. If there were only one rose in the world I should want it to be Albertine, that glorious cascade of the pinkest pink. If I had a very high wall, I should like it tumbling over every inch of it.

SUSAN HILL,
FROM *"THE MAGIC APPLE TREE"*

⊰ ⊱

A rose is so unnecessarily beautiful.

PAM BROWN, b.1928

...roses are the most seductive and
breathtakingly beautiful of all flowers, creamy
or silvery white, shell or blush or faded pink,
deepest blood and purple-red, lemon and
sunshine and moonlight yellow, tight or flat
open, inward or outward curving, frilled or
plain, grey or budded or pale green or bronze or
dark of foliage, upright, spreading, bushy habit,
thick-set or delicate, gaudy or subtle, blowsy or
modest.

SUSAN HILL,
FROM *"THROUGH THE GARDEN GATE"*

Oh whence could such a plant have sprung?
The earth produced an infant flower.
Which spring with blushing tinctures drest,
The gods beheld this brilliant birth,
And hailed the rose, the boon on earth.

ANACREON (C.570-C.475 B.C.)

A <u>ROSE FOR PEACE</u>

A rose is an argument. It proclaims the triumph of beauty over brutality, of gentleness over violence, of the ephemeral over the lasting, and of the universal over the particular. The same rose bursts into bloom on the North Cape and in the Sahara desert.

ALAIN MEILLAND

Just as rewarding and even more heart-warming than all the medals, the awards, were the letters that now began to pour in from all parts of the world. It was as if people everywhere, utterly sick and weary of brutality, violence, senseless destruction, felt their hearts lift again to see so lovely and generous a rose [Peace] with so kind and welcome a name.

...nine years after the Americans gave it its lovely name, it was estimated that thirty million "Peace" rose-bushes were flowering all over the world; and Francis [Meilland] wrote in his diary: "How rewarding it is for an ordinary working gardener to know his rose is growing in cottage gardens, in the grounds of mansions, around churches, and mosques and hospitals, and in public parks; and to think that so many people are now seeing the rose he alone once saw in his mind as he strove to create it."

ANTONIA RIDGE,
FROM *"FOR LOVE OF A ROSE"*

One comes back to those old-fashioned roses as one does to old music and poetry. A garden needs old association, old fragrances, as a home needs things that have been lived with.

FROM *"THE ROSA ANNUAL"*, 1928

❧ ❧

There are manufactured roses - long-stemmed and perfect, thornless and free of both scent and greenfly. They are predestined to live their hour in dressing rooms, in boudoirs. They are extravagance made tangible, shielded by cellophane. They die before they open.

Real roses tumble their petals onto piano tops and carpets. They have thorns and too many leaves and smell of summer gardens. They come with kisses.

CLARA ORTEGA, b.1955

❧ ❧

I like old roses best. Untidy, tousled, simple, heavy-scented, thorned. Comfortable company on a drowsing summer's day.

MARION GARRETTY, b.1917

❧ ❧

What other planet smells of roses?

HELEN THOMSON, b.1943

⊰ ⊱

When roses are in full bloom, the most magical place to be is in a rose garden. There the senses are bombarded with the glorious colours, shapes and perfumes of the flowers. And we can easily enjoy all of these attributes indoors. It takes no more than a single rose in a vase, a bowl of fragrant potpourri, a deliciously scented perfume or soap, or a delectable sweet to take us back into that wonderfully perfumed garden at any time we wish.

MALCOLM HILLIER

⊰ ⊱

It is strange that the chemist, with all his scientific wisdom, has not yet been able to produce a sweeter smell than the perfume of a cabbage rose on a hot summer's day.

PRINCESS GRACE OF MONACO (1929-1982),
FROM *"MY BOOK OF FLOWERS"*

⊰ ⊱

We all know persons who are affected for better or for worse by certain odours.... Over and over again I have experienced the quieting influence of Rose scent upon a disturbed state of mind, feeling the troubled condition smoothing out before I realized that Roses were in the room, or near at hand.

LOUISE BEEBE WILDER

A HEALING CALM

...the perfume of the rose is as important to the health of the mind as food is to the body. The rose grower will rarely suffer from bouts of depression while able to get around the garden, even in an invalid's chair, for the beauty and fragrance of the blooms act as an antidote to a tired mind.

ROY GENDERS,
FROM *"THE ROSE. A COMPLETE HANDBOOK"*

A rose smiled at me from the hedge,
My heart responded happily.
And something nudged me from life's edge
As who was rose, and who was me?
Between ourselves there's little but
A subtle change of chemistry.

JACK HARKNESS

They that have roses never need bread.

DOROTHY PARKER (1839-1967)

There is no healing coolness like that of the petals of a rose.

CHARLOTTE GRAY, b.1937

...who can walk among roses in a garden and not feel refreshed by their beauty and fragrance.

ROY GENDERS,
FROM *"THE ROSE. A COMPLETE HANDBOOK"*

SUMMER DAYS

Summer perfected is a drowse of bees
and roses.

HELEN THOMSON, b.1943

All who garden will have special memories
of summer days made brighter by a
pageant of roses growing over trellis
or pergola, across a wall or twining
themselves up and through the
branches of a tree, offering flowers which
belong to warm sunny days and
gladsome things.

GEOFFREY SMITH,
FROM *"A PASSION FOR PLANTS"*

I have this sense that if the rose were to vanish,
there would be no more beautiful summer days.

MARION GARRETTY, b.1917

THE TRUE ROSE GROWER

He who would have beautiful Roses in
his garden must have beautiful Roses
in his heart. He must love them well and always....
He must have not only the glowing admiration,
the enthusiasm, and the passion, but
the tenderness, the thoughtfulness, the
reverence, the watchfulness of love.... He is
loyal and devoted ever, in storm-fraught
or in sunny days; not only the first upon a
summer's morning to gaze admiringly on
glowing charms, but the first, when leaves
fall and winds are chill, to protect against
cruel frost. As with smitten bachelor or
steadfast mate the lady of his love is lovely ever,
so to the true Rose-grower must the Rose-tree
be always a thing of beauty. To others,
when its flowers have faded, it may be
worthless as a hedgerow thorn: to him, in every
phase, it is precious.

S. REYNOLDS HOLE,
FROM *"A BOOK ABOUT ROSES"*

WHAT IS SO VERY SPECIAL?

What is so special about a rose that it seems far more than a flower? Perhaps it is the mystery it has gathered through the ages. Perhaps it is the joy that it continues to give. Humans have constantly used it to transmit sentiments that they lack words to express, for the rose is different. It is one of the great visual contributions to human life. Its beauty is remarkable - from the wild rose to the immaculate beauty of the hybrid tea.

**PRINCESS GRACE OF MONACO (1929-1982),
FROM *"MY BOOK OF FLOWERS"***

Wandering amongst shrub roses in full bloom, enjoying the quality of the flowers and inhaling the scent they distil, is a mind-beguiling business. Trying to compare flower shape and scent usually leads to a splendid extravagance born of mental intoxication.

GEOFFREY SMITH

THE VELVET ROSE

The Velvet Rose. What a combination of words!
One almost suffocates in their soft depths,
as though one sank into a bed of rose-petals,
all thorns ideally stripped away. It is
improbable that we shall ever lie on a bed
of roses, unless we are very decadent and
also very rich, but we can imagine ourselves
doing so when we hold a single rose close
to our eyes and absorb it in an intimate way
into our private heart.

VITA SACKVILLE-WEST (1892-1962)

But when...thy roses came to me
My sense with their deliciousness was spell'd:
Soft voices had they, that with tender plea
Whisper'd of peace, and truth, and friendliness
unquell'd.

JOHN KEATS (1795-1821),
FROM *"TO A FRIEND WHO SENT ME SOME ROSES"*

THE LOVELY ROSE

There are so many unexpected
moments of rare beauty associated
with roses. Even when the flowers
are hidden in fading light their
perfume is held on the air: an
all-pervading reminder of the
loveliness that will be there for us
to enjoy through long, sunlit days.
Though time may erode all things,
yet the rose continues to build truth
on legend until the position this flower
holds in public esteem is assured for
as long as there are gardens and
gardeners to care for it.

GEOFFREY SMITH,
FROM *"A PASSION FOR PLANTS"*